Deconstructing Production Music for TV

SECRETS BEHIND WRITING SUCCESSFUL MUSIC CUES

by Steve Barden

To access audio visit:
www.halleonard.com/mylibrary

"Enter Code"
"1882-0406-5721-1949"

ISBN 978-1-57424-402-1
SAN 683-8022

Cover by James Creative Group

P.O. Box 17878 - Anaheim Hills, CA 92817

www.centerstream-usa.com | centerstrm@aol.com | 714-779-9390

Table of Contents

Introduction 4

Song 1 - Beyond the Stars (adventure) 5

Song 2 - Ring of Power (trailer/epic) 13

Song 3 - Fairy Tale Romance (romantic) 23

Song 4 - Angels and Demons (fantasy adventure) 32

Song 5 - No Mountain Too High (uplifting/epic) 39

Song 6 - Silly Willy (cartoon) 49

Song 7 - At the Casino (jazz/dramedy) 56

Song 8 - On the Move (dramedy) 63

Song 9 - Countdown to Zero Hour (dramedy) 72

Acknowledgements 80

About the Author 81

Introduction

A major portion of my music composing these days is writing *production music*. There are many reasons for this:

- You can earn good money from it for years to come in back-end performance royalties
- It's extremely creative
- You get to decide *what kind* of music you want to create and *when* you want to create it
- You can choose to work with other musicians or entirely by yourself

This book is about composing music for production music libraries that will be used, primarily, on television. This is not the same as *film scoring*, that is, scoring-to-picture. What's the difference? Scoring-to-picture is writing music to specifically accompany a film (or television show, or documentary, etc.). As a composer you will have the knowledge of what's going to happen on the screen, when it's going to happen, and what emotion you will need to convey.

Writing production music is writing blindly. You have no idea how your music will be used. Production music is *reusable*. You might find your same music cue being used on many different projects. Scoring-to-picture is designed to be used for a very specific need. That's why when writing production music your goal is to stick to a singular emotion. Changing up emotions within a music cue will make it difficult to get your music placed. And no placements mean no money!

In my book, *Writing Production Music for TV: The Road to Success* (Centerstream, 2017), I describe in great detail the ins and outs of the production music industry: everything from working with music libraries, to collaboration, to contracts, and more. But very little is devoted to the actual mechanics of music composition. That's what this book series is all about. I am presenting you with a set of music scores with detailed analysis about why this music will work in a production music environment.

Each score will be prefaced with a description of the cue explaining things like:

- The structure of the music
- An explanation of the chord progression
- Melodic consideration
- Instrumentation choices
- Style/Genre
- Intended usage and emotion depicted
- Sound libraries used
- Analysis of various bars/sections of the score
- Why this cue works

Production music is intended to be functional. It is never meant to overshadow the visuals on the screen. It needs to serve a very specific purpose and convey a singular emotion. Melody is often a lower priority to the overall vibe of the cue. As long as it serves its purpose by supporting the scene then you've done your job. It's not how great a composer you are or how many notes you can write. It's never about "chops." Save that for the concert stage!

Is my way the only way to compose production music? Of course not. Everyone will develop their own voice, their own style, their own sound. Your takeaway from this book is the understanding of why the music I'm presenting works. Your job going forward is to translate this information into your own amazing compositions.

This edition of the series will focus on orchestral compositions in several popular production music genres such as Dramedy, Epic, and Romantic.

Let's get started and happy composing!

Beyond the Stars

Tempo: 72 bpm

Key: F major

Track 1 - Beyond the Stars.mp3

Beyond the Stars is an orchestral theme in the style - both melodically and harmonically - of Jerry Goldsmith and John Williams. These legendary composers have set the standard of what to expect when scoring a science fiction space film.

The structure of this cue is technically in A-B form; however, it could be considered as A-A since the thematic material continues to vary its original theme in each section. The cue is set at a moderate tempo of 72 bpm.

The cue opens quietly with the piano playing open fifths (F and C) while the violins follow suit an octave higher. The violins are muted, and the first violins are also playing harmonics. Windchimes can also be heard lightly in the background. The lack of the 3rd in the chord gives it a neutral sound. It is neither major nor minor. This gives the piece an ethereal quality.

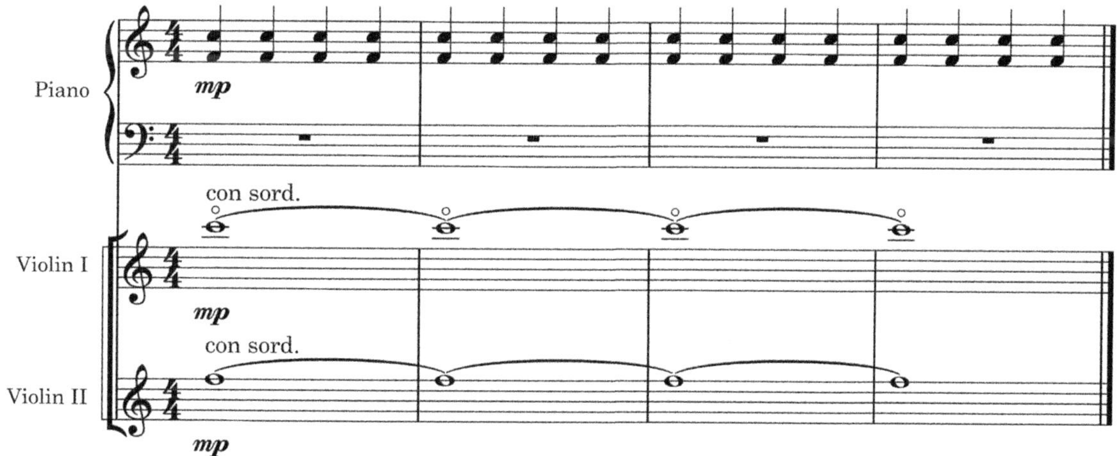

Fig 1

The first melodic theme begins in bar 2 by the clarinets, French horns, and violas, and repeated (echoed) in bar 5 by the cellos doubled by the bassoon:

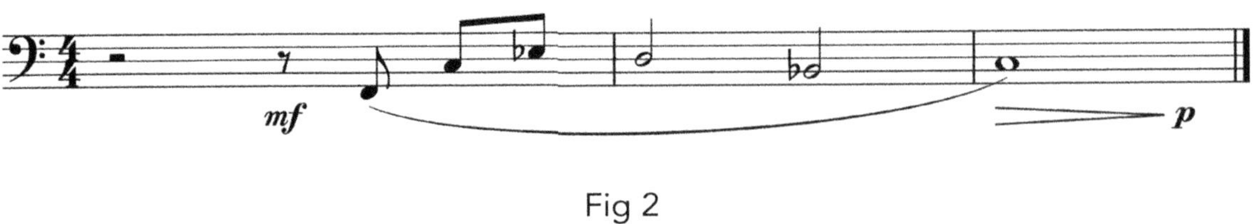

Fig 2

The french horns in the opening phrase suggest a majestic tone. Although the score indicates a standard grouping of 4 horns in unison, the recording takes advantage of the CineBrass 12 Horns patch for that bigger-than-life sound. The 3-note motif (the opening 3 notes) ascending from the root to the fifth to the minor 7th will be repeated throughout the cue.

This sets up the main theme that will be varied both rhythmically and melodically as the cue develops. As the high woodwinds enter in bar 7, the shape - the up and down motion - of the opening melody is varied:

Fig 3

In bar 9, the trumpets and horns play in octaves and reinforces the opening 3-note motif:

Fig 4

The "B" section begins at bar 14 (letter B) where we introduce a playful passage with the violas and cellos playing a light and fast pizzicato pattern...

Fig 5

...while the violins and clarinets continue with the melodic theme...

Fig 6

...and we introduce a counter melody with the horns:

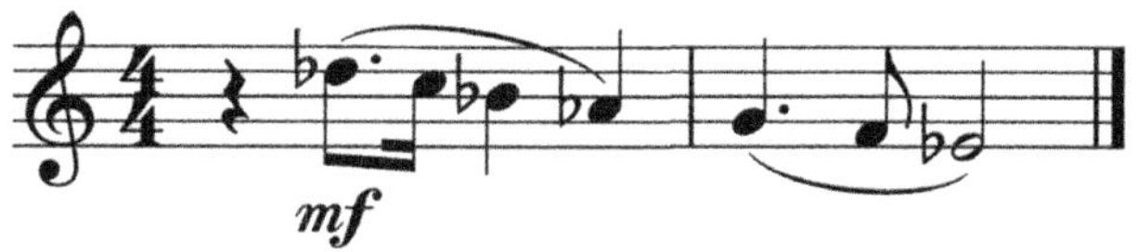

Fig 7

Bar 18 (letter C) begins the final passage. At bar 23 the repeated ostinato pattern of the clarinets (along with a slower variation by the violas and cellos at the same time) gives this space theme its secret sauce: The G# (#11) of the D major chord defines the lydian mode that is highly cinematic and typical of this genre.

Fig 8

Virtual Instruments

For this recording I utilized the following instruments:

Spitfire woodwinds (piccolo, flutes, clarinets, bassoon)
Berlin woodwinds (oboe)
CineBrass (12 French horns, trumpets, trombones)
CinePerc (timpani, cymbals, piatti, windchimes, bass drum, glockenspiel, celeste)
CineHarp
CinePiano
Spitfire Symphonic Strings

Recorded in StaffPad, mixed in Cubase

Usage

How might a cue like this be used? The feel of the piece is a flowing, pastoral journey. It could, by design, be used to set the tone of a story that takes place in outer space. It would also sit nicely behind nature environments: forests, mountains, oceans, etc.

Metadata

The melody is not obtrusive and could easily sit behind dialogue or narration. There is a calmness that makes it useful in many settings. When creating metadata for the cue to help identify the music's characteristics you might include descriptions such as:

Blissful, celestial, confident, heavenly, majestic, soaring, uplifting, etc.

Beyond the Stars

Composed and Orchestrated by
Steve Barden

10
11
12
13
14
15
B ♩= 82
Piccolo
2 Flutes in C
Oboe
2 Clarinets in B♭
Bassoon
4 Fr Horns in F
3 Trumpets in B♭
con sord
Sus Cymbals
CinePerc Piatti
Glockenspiel in C
Windchimes
Harp
gliss.
Piano
Violin 1
Violin 2
Viola
pizz.
Violoncello
pizz.
Contrabass in C
pizz.

16
17
18
19
20
21
22
C ♩= 72
Piccolo
2 Flutes in C
Oboe
2 Clarinets in B♭
Bassoon
4 Fr Horns in F
3 Trumpets in B♭
2 Trombones
Timpani
Sus Cymbals
Glockenspiel in C
Harp
Piano
Violin 1
Violin 2
Viola
Violoncello
Contrabass in C
mp
a2
open
mf
p
f
gliss.
arco

23 24 25 26 27 28

2 Flutes in C

Oboe

2 Clarinets in B♭

Bassoon

4 Fr Horns in F

3 Trumpets in B♭

2 Trombones

Timpani

Sus Cymbals

CinePerc Piatti

Glockenspiel in C

Harp

Celesta

Piano

23 24 25 26 27 28

Violin 1

Violin 2

Viola

Violoncello

Contrabass in C

Ring of Power

Tempo: 128 bpm

Key: Eb major

 Track 2 - Ring of Power.mp3

Ring of Power falls under the category of *Epic* music. This genre stands on its own with a huge fan base, it also forms the current style of film trailer music.

Epic music is typically a combination of orchestral instrumentation integrated with hybrid synthesized instruments and additional sound design such as risers, downers, whooshes, swipes, and huge drum hits.

This particular cue will consist of orchestral instruments only, although you could easily spice it up with the hybrid sounds mentioned above. In fact, providing alternate versions of the cue with and without these hybrid elements is highly recommended as it will increase your chances of having the cue getting used.

The form of the cue is a repeated 8-bar pattern. In the key of Eb and at a tempo of 128 bpm, the chord progression is Eb - Bb - Cm - Ab. In music theory that is the I - V - vi - IV pattern. This chord progression is extremely common in trailer music and has been used (and overused) to death. But it still works quite well and that's why I've used it in this example.

This 8-bar pattern repeats a total of eight times, each time introducing a new sound with ever increasing volume and energy. This is a critical concept in trailer and epic music: build and build the cue until it is ready to explode in excitement. Looking at the waveform below, it's obvious how the cue will build and build to a climax before finally returning to calm at the very end.

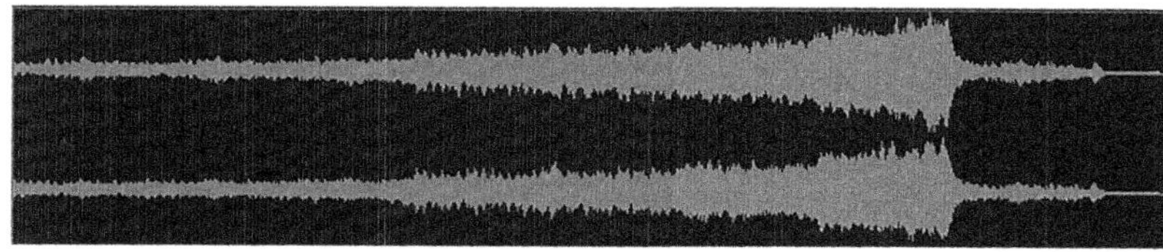

Rehearsal marking A begins with the piano by itself, defining the chord progression, each chord lasting two bars.

Fig 1

At letter B we add violas playing a staccatissimo ostinato pattern. This repetitive pattern is extremely typical of trailer and epic music and will continue for the duration of the cue.

Fig 2

As the piano and violas continue, the rest of the strings enter at letter C playing a simple pad.

Fig 3

Next, at letter D, we introduce drums playing a basic rock beat. The entrance of the drums is the beginning of the buildup of the intensity of the cue.

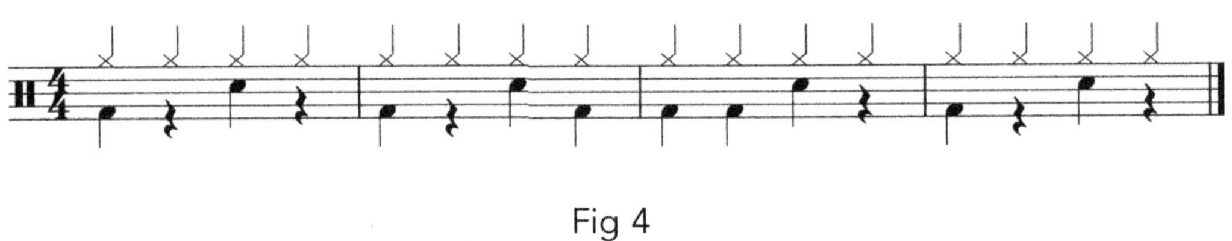

Fig 4

Next, we introduce low brass starting at letter E. We start with a tuba and will be accompanied by the trombones in the next section. The tuba, with its velvety tone, adds a low bass sound without overwhelming the cue. By adding the trombones at letter F, we increase the intensity. The trombones have more of a bite than the tuba.

Fig 5

At the same time as the tuba entrance, we also bring on the big drum hits. "Big drums" are one of the stylistic requirements of trailer and epic music. Drum hits can never be too big. It is recommended to layer several types of drums (taikos, tom toms, frame drums, surdos, etc.) in order to build up the necessary explosions.

The part itself should be uncomplicated. Simple rhythms are all that is necessary. In fact, the more complicated the rhythmic pattern the more likely the drums will blur and lose the clarity of having the drum hits in the first place.

Fig 6

Up to this point, the dynamics of the cue have remained at mezzo-forte (mf). But the simple addition of more and more instruments as the piece progresses increases volume and intensity without even trying. But by the time we reach letter F we bring in the choir at a dynamic of forte (f).

The choir initially begins with just the women (sopranos and altos).

Fig 7

By the next section, letter G, we also add the men (tenors and basses) to the choir and increase the volume to fortissimo (ff).

Fig 8

At the same time as the entrance of the men at letter G we add the French horns playing a melody. Rhythmically it matches the violin melody but stands on its own. French horns are another one of the staple instruments in trailer and epic music. The nasal brassiness of the instrument in this register gives it a noble and majestic sound which brings the cue to a much-needed climax.

Fig 9

As the French horns reach their high note the cue hits an abrupt stop. The piano continues as it did in the intro but this time accompanied lightly by the violins fading to near silence.

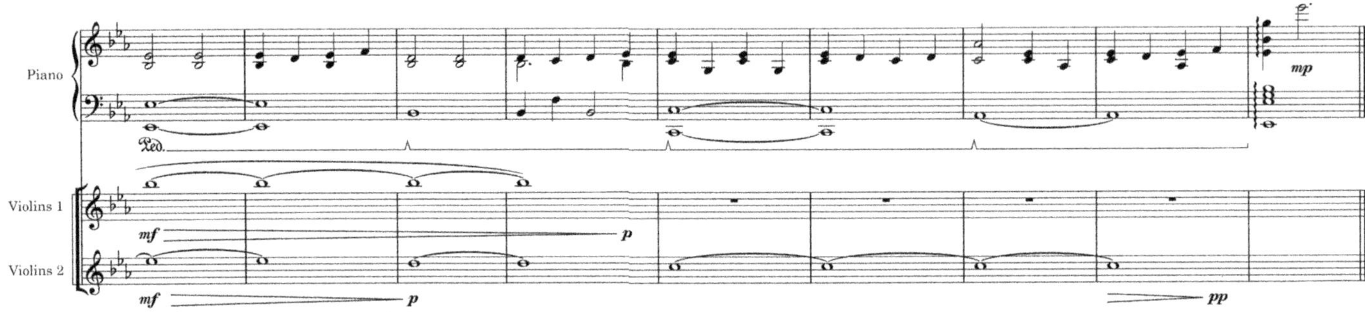

Fig 10

A lot happens over the course of the cue. Here is an overview of the arrangement to break down its components:

A - Piano introduction

B - Piano + viola ostinato

C - Piano + viola ostinato + string pad

D - Piano + viola ostinato + string pad + violin melody + drums

E - Piano + viola ostinato + string pad + violin melody + drums + low brass + big drum hits

F - Piano + viola ostinato + string pad + violin melody + drums + low brass + big drum hits + choir

G - Piano + viola ostinato + string pad + violin melody + drums + low brass + big drum hits + more choir + Fr horn melody

H - Piano outro + diminishing violins

Virtual Instruments

For this recording I utilized the following instruments:

Berlin woodwinds (flute, English horn)
CineBrass (12 french horns, bass trombone, tuba)
CinePerc (cymbals, piatti)
CinePerc (timpani, concert toms, surdos, monster low hits, frame drums)
StaffPad drum kit and pop kit
Metropolis Ark 1 drum kit
Heavyocity Damage (Studio Armageddon Ens, Big Organo Kit)
Voxos choir
CinePiano
Berlin strings

Recorded in StaffPad, mixed in Cubase

Usage

How might a cue like this be used? The music is a journey, from understated simplicity to unrestrained glory. Examples might include: a montage sequence spanning someone's life; a soldier returning from war; an athlete from training to winning the gold medal...anything that tells a story. The possibilities are endless.

Metadata

When creating metadata for the cue to help identify the music's characteristics you might include descriptions such as:

Hopeful, majestic, noble, soaring, triumphant, uplifting, etc.

Ring of Power

Composed and Orchestrated by
Steve Barden

29
30
31
32
E
33
34
35
Flute
Tuba
mf
Cymbals
mf
Piatti
f
Timpani
f
Toms
mf
Drum Kit
Piano
Ped.
Violins 1
Violins 2
Violas
Cellos
Basses

36
37
38
39
40
F
41
42
Flute
B Trombone
Tuba
Piatti
Timpani
Toms
Drum Kit
Choir
Piano
Violins 1
Violins 2
Violas
Cellos
Basses
f
mf
(Ped.)
Ped.

43
44
45
46
47
48
49
G
Flute
Eng Horn in F
F Horn in F
B Trombone
Tuba
Piatti
Timpani
Toms
Drum Kit
Choir
Piano
Violins 1
Violins 2
Violas
Cellos
Basses
ff
f

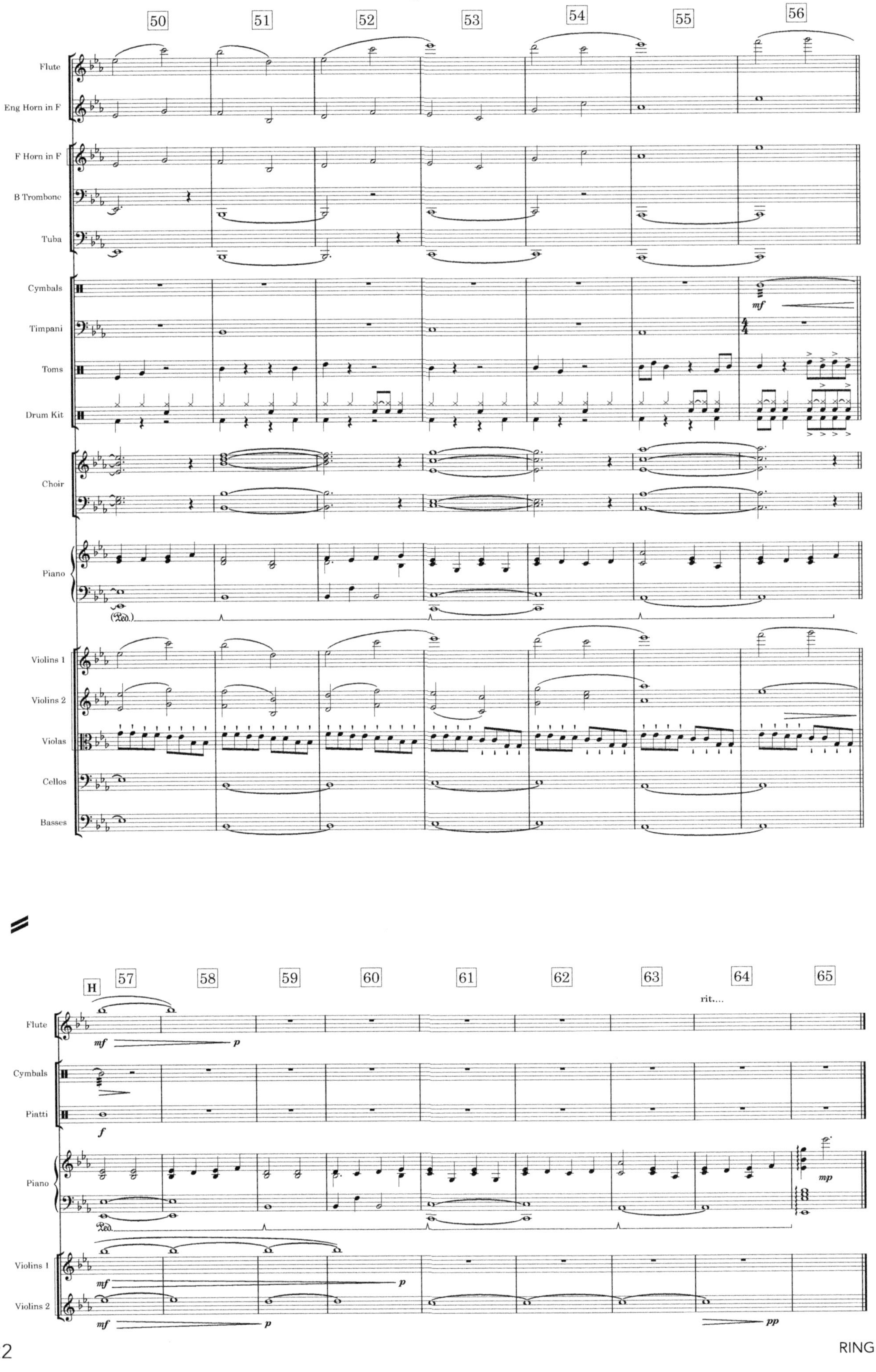

50 51 52 53 54 55 56

Flute
Eng Horn in F
F Horn in F
B Trombone
Tuba
Cymbals
mf
Timpani
Toms
Drum Kit
Choir
Piano
(Ped.)
Violins 1
Violins 2
Violas
Cellos
Basses

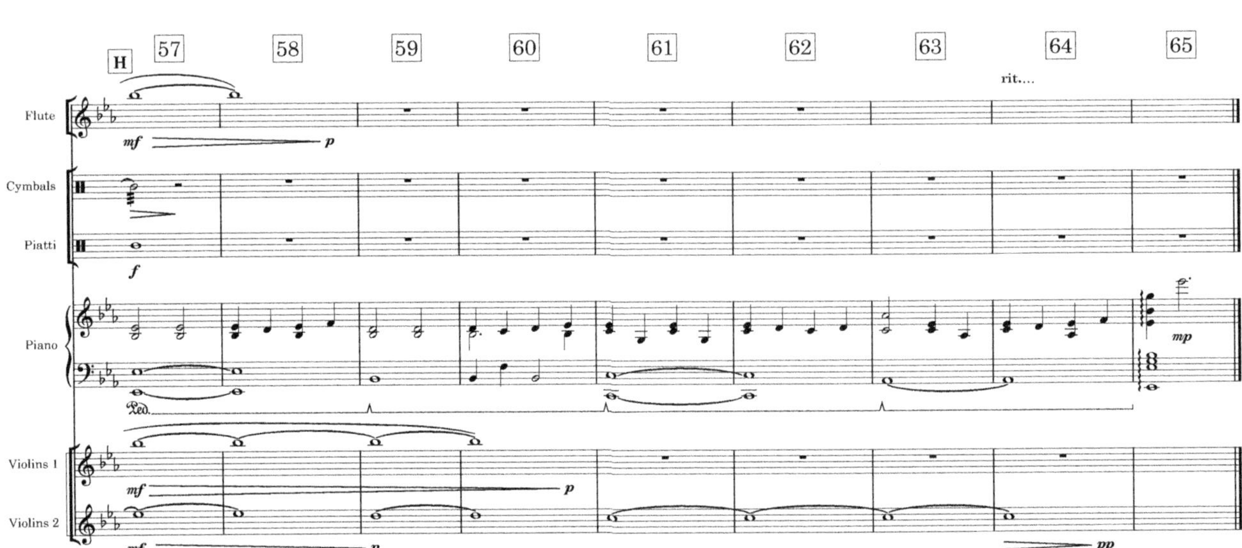

Fairy Tale Romance

Tempo: 80 bpm

Key: A major

Track 3 - Fairy Tale Romance.mp3

Production music quite often requires music cues to be no more than 90 seconds to two minutes in length. Occasionally you will be asked to provide even longer cues, sometimes in the three-minute range. *Fairy Tale Romance* is an example of constructing a piece that fits this requirement. The cue is set at a moderate tempo of 80 bpm in the key of A major.

Rather than stating a theme as the A section, varying it with a B section, and restating it in a final A section (A-B-A), this cue takes the essence of the theme and builds upon it to extend to the full three minutes. You will see that it is consistent thematically throughout while changing the orchestration to make it interesting from start to finish.

The overall feel is that of a lush, large orchestral movement, one that might be characteristic of a Disney princess film. The cue opens with solo piano, defining the rhythmic structure of the melody. Bar 2 (eighth-, quarter-, eighth-, and half-note) is the common thread throughout the piece, even when the melody varies.

Fig 1

After the piano intro, the strings will enter. The first violins (doubled by the flutes) perform the melody while the rest of the string section settle for a supportive, warm pad underneath. Notice that rhythmically the new melody is the same pattern as the piano in bar 2. This rhythm will persist throughout the cue.

Fig 2

At letter C, we introduce a brief harmonic change to introduce the next section at letter D.

Fig 3

Letter D now introduces a new thematic section. Although the melody is different, the harmonies in the first two bars are identical to what we've seen so far: A - C#m7/G# - F#m7 - A/E. But now we give our ears a break with a G major chord in the third bar (bar 26) before returning to the tonic A major.

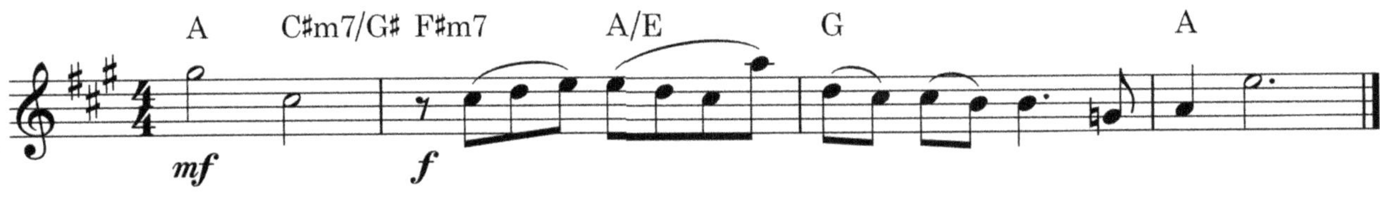

Fig 4

With the G major chord in the third bar, we maintain the key signature's C# melody which puts it in a lydian mode, and as noted elsewhere in this book, is very cinematic! Harmonically the cue stays in the key of A major throughout with very little deviation, so the introduction of the G major chord really makes it stand out.

Next, at letter E we introduce one more interlude that will set up the final section. This is the only section where harmonically and melodically it stands on its own. There's nothing wrong with doing this. Color-wise, the instrumentation is consistent with the rest of the composition. It also acts as a bridge, similar to what we'd do in a B section of a typical A-B-A form. It gives our ear a break and brings it home when we return to the main melody one last time.

Fig 5

By including harp, choir, celesta, and glockenspiel, the music maintains that "magical" sound often found in this type of score.

Virtual Instruments

For this recording I utilized the following instruments:

Spitfire woodwinds (cor anglais)

Berlin woodwinds (flutes, oboes, clarinets, bassoons)

Berlin brass (horns and trumpets)

CineBrass (trombones and tuba)

CinePerc (timpani, tubular bells, piatti, cymbals, glockenspiel, celeste)

Voxos choir

CinePiano

Spitfire Symphonic Strings

Recorded in StaffPad, mixed in Cubase

Usage

How might a cue like this be used? At stated earlier, this would fit a setting that supports romance, such as the Disney princess example. Any type of romantic film such as a Hallmark movie (their trademark!), a jewelry store commercial, even the love between a child and a puppy is the target for this style cue.

The sentiment is mistakenly heartwarming. By keeping the melody simple and flowing it cannot be interpreted any other way. Of course, it doesn't hurt to have huge harp glissandos and a choir giving that angelic quality.

Metadata

When creating metadata for the cue to help identify the music's characteristics you might include descriptions such as:

Beautiful, enchanted, joyful, loving, sweet, tender, etc.

Fairy Tale Romance

Composed and Orchestrated by
Steve Barden

D

21 22 23 24 25 26 27

Fl. 1.2
Picc.
Picc.
To Fl.
Cl. in B♭ 1.2
a 2
Bsn 1 2
F. Hn in F 1.2
a 2
F. Hn in F 3.4
a 2
Tbn.
B. Tbn.
Tba
Cymbals
Glock.
S.
A.
Pno
Vln 1
Vln 2
pizz.
Vla
pizz.
Vc.
pizz.
D. B.
pizz.
arco
pizz.

E
Fl. 1 2
Fl. 3
C. A.
Cl. in B♭ 1.2
Bsn 1 2
Tpt in B♭ 1.2
Tpt in B♭ 3
Tbn.
B. Tbn.
Tba
Timp.
Tub. Bells
Glock.
S.
A.
Hp
Vln 1
Vln 2
Vla
Vc.
D. B.
a 2
Fl.
gliss.
con sord.
normal
arco

Fl. 1.2
Fl. 3
Ob. 1.2
C. A.
Cl. in B♭ 1.2
Bsn 1.2
F. Hn in F 1.2
F. Hn in F 3.4
Tpt in B♭ 1 2
Tpt in B♭ 3
Tbn.
B. Tbn.
Tba
Timp.
Glock.
S.
A.
Hp
Cel.
Vln 1
Vln 2
Vla
Vc.
D. B.
F
a 2
gliss.
D♯
8va

Fl. 1 2
Fl. 3
Ob. 1 2
C. A.
Bsn 1 2
F. Hn in F 1 2
F. Hn in F 3 4
Tpt in B♭ 1.2.3
Tbn.
B. Tbn.
Tba
Timp.
Piatti
Glock.
S.
A.
Pno
Vln 1
Vln 2
Vla
Vc.
D. B.
48
49
50
51
52
53
54
55
a 2
a 3
1.2. a 2
mf
mp
p
f
ff
fff
tr

Angels and Demons

Tempo: 112 bpm

Key: C minor

Track 4 - Angels and Demons.mp3

Inspired by Howard Shore's work on Lord of the Rings, *Angels and Demons* is characteristic of that style of writing. It makes use of the low instruments in the orchestra, or by playing in their lowest registers. This cue features 2 clarinets, 2 bassoons, 4 horns, 2 trombones, bass trombone, tuba, choir (with solo alto voice), glockenspiel, and strings.

The cue is set at a moderate tempo of 112 bpm, although it feels slower due to the fact that most notes played are whole and half notes. Putting the piece in a minor key gives it a darker tone. The key signature is Cm, however, the harmonic structure has the piece jumping around to some distant keys such as Abm and D major.

The abrupt change in keys gives the cue a very cinematic flavor and typical of this genre. Covering the voicings shown below, the orchestra plays this figure tutti. It is a very dark and rich tone. Rhythmically, it is a short note followed by a long note. Considering the tempo, half notes feel very short. It could very well have been written at half tempo, 66 bpm, with the first note being a quarter note followed by a dotted half note. The reason I chose to represent it in this fashion is that I want a beat of silence before the next chord and this is more readable. Either way, the result would be the same.

Fig 1

Notice there is no percussion throughout the piece, with the exception of the glockenspiel at the end. The opening eight bars (letter A) establishes the tonal color of the piece. At letter B we introduce a female solo vocalist. The part is ad-libbed, not strictly in time. The soulfulness of the performance adds a tremendous amount to the overall texture.

Fig 2

At letter C the solo voice is replaced by a solo French horn. The melody is simple - as is everything about this piece.

Fig 3

At letter D the solo female voice returns, and we add basso profundo male voices supporting the rhythm of the orchestra. The intensity of the piece is growing. Next, at letter E, all four French horns join together in a simple whole-note melody (figure 4). At this point they are playing forte.

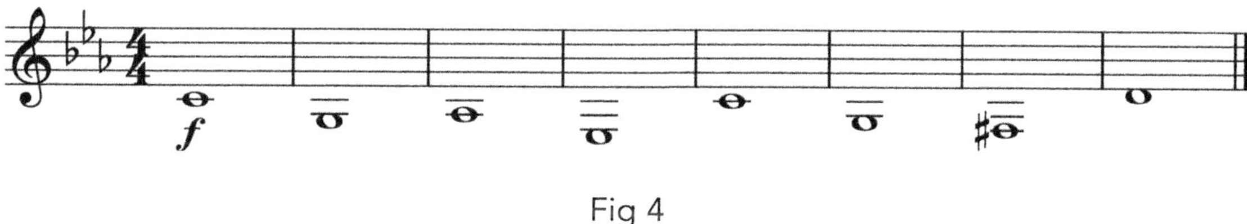

Fig 4

The four horns and first violins (an octave higher) continue with the melody at letter F, but now the rhythms change by adding eighth notes for variety.

Fig 5

The orchestra builds to a climax at the end of this section. As the French horns hit the high D note everything drops out except a boys choir and the high strings holding out chords lasting two measures each. The glockenspiel adds a single note to the beginning of each two-measure grouping.

A solo cello joins at the fourth measure of letter G (bar 52) by playing a mournful melody. The piece concludes on a long and fading Cm chord to silence.

Virtual Instruments

For this recording I utilized the following instruments:

CineOrch orchestral chord pads
CineBrass solo horn
CineBrass 12-horns
CineBrass low brass pads
CinePerc glockenspiel
Metropolis Ark 1&2 choirs (women, men, profundo bass)
Voxos boys choir
Heavyocity Gravity Pack: Vocalise (vocal phrases)
Berlin strings violins
Albion 5 Tundra strings
Tina Guo solo cello

Recorded and mixed in Cubase

Usage

How might a cue like this be used? The texture is dark and brooding. This would easily fit in a film trailer opening sequence. Documentaries, depending on the subject matter, would benefit from the piece as it is textural and not overly melodic.

Metadata

The melody is not obtrusive and could easily sit behind dialogue or narration. When creating metadata for the cue to help identify the music's characteristics you might include descriptions such as:

Atmospheric, dark, eerie, foreboding, haunting, mournful, solemn, etc.

Angels and Demons

Composed and Orchestrated by
Steve Barden

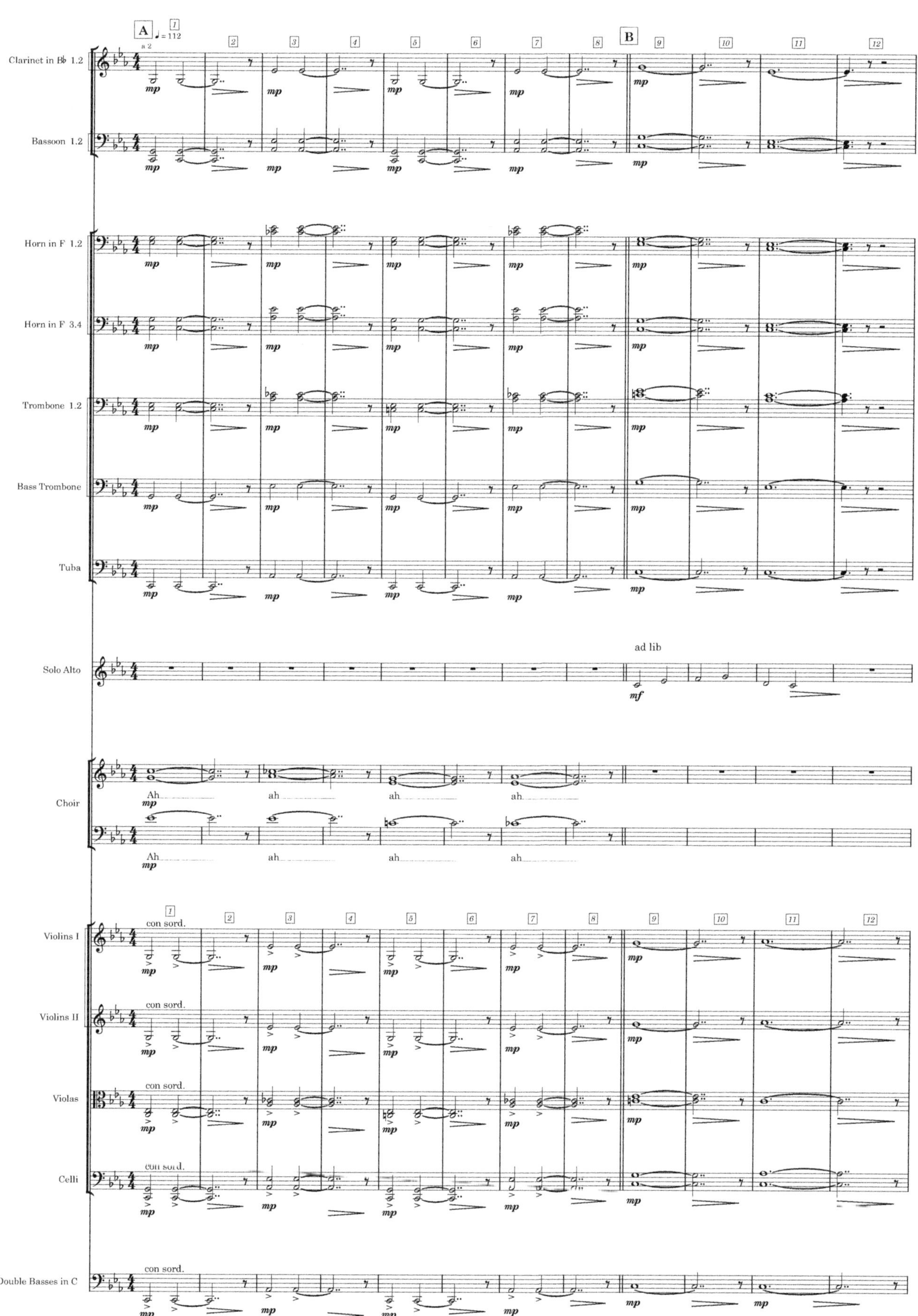

Clarinet in B♭ 1.2
Bassoon 1.2
Horn in F 1.2
Horn in F 3.4
Trombone 1.2
Bass Trombone
Tuba
Solo Alto
Choir
Ah
ah
ah
ah
Violins I
Violins II
Violas
Celli
DB in C

D
E
Clarinet in B♭ 1.2
Bassoon 1.2
Horn in F 1 2
Horn in F 3.4
Trombone 1.2
Bass Trombone
Tuba
Solo Alto
Choir
Ma ma Ma ma Ma ma Ma ma
Ah ah ah ah ah
Violins I
ord.
Violins II
Violas
Celli
DB in C

F
G
Clarinet in B♭ 1.2
Bassoon 1.2
Horn in F 1.2
Horn in F 3.4
Trombone 1.2
Bass Trombone
Tuba
Glock in C
Choir
Violins I
Violins II
Violas
Celli
DB in C
a 2
mf
f
p
mp
ppp
ah
Ah

No Mountain Too High

Tempo: 132 bpm

Key: C major

Track 5 - No Mountain Too High.mp3

The primary goal for *No Mountain Too High* is to be uplifting. Set at 132 bpm, the meter is set at 3/4. All of the other music in this volume is set at 4/4 which is the most commonly used time signature used in production music.

A time signature of 3/4 gives it a waltz-like feel. It flows. It dances. At this tempo you might think it was written in either 6/8 or 12/8 time. This gives it the necessary drive to feel uplifting. It's no wonder that the song *Happy Birthday* is set at 3/4.

The chord progression follows the common vi - IV - I - V pattern. The key is C so the chords progress Am - F - C - G. We change key at letter D. This could be considered the B section. The progression is exactly the same (vi - IV - I - V) but now we've modulated up a minor third to Eb. The chords progress Cm - Ab - Eb - Bb. Modulating up a minor third is a very common pattern in film scoring and will sound very cinematic if you do that. We will return to the key of C at letter E.

The cue begins with the piano playing the chord progression for two bars each (six beats). The piano is accompanied by low strings.

Fig 1

Halfway through letter A, a solo cello is introduced playing a plaintive melody. The melody is rather sparse, but is preferable in production music as to not overwhelm the scene.

Fig 2

The cue will build in intensity with each new section. Letter B introduces the viola ostinato pattern to give it that driving beat. This is the same type of ostinato that is found in *Epic*-style cues.

Fig 3

Letter C brings in a soaring melody played by the first violins and the cellos. The French horns and low brass fill out the texture with a chord pad.

Fig 4

More additions starting at letter D. This is where we modulate to the key of Eb. The French horn section plays a melody that is similar to the violins/cellos melody, but even simpler.

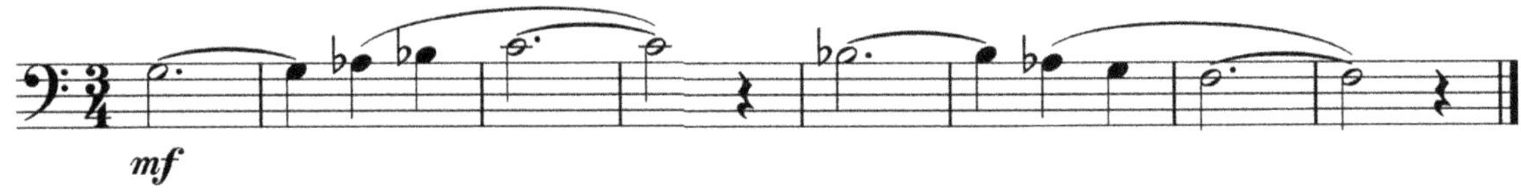

Fig 5

The second violins take over the ostinato pattern from the violas but play an octave higher.

Fig 6

Drums have also been added playing a driving beat that is supported by the cellos playing divisi. The texture of the chords is thickened by the addition of the 9th in the chords by the cellos in every other pair of bars.

Fig 7

Letter E returns to the key of C and we add flutes and a piccolo playing a complimentary ostinato pattern to what both the second violins and violas are playing (an octave apart). The woodwinds add a beautiful brightness to the piece at this point.

Fig 8

For the big finish, a new melody based on the melodic movement we heard in letter C by the French horns, trumpets, and first violins bring the piece to a climax. We've now increased dynamics to forte (f).

Fig 9

At letter F we bring it home by dropping out everybody except the piano and high strings. This is a recap of the introduction.

Virtual Instruments

For this recording I utilized the following instruments:

Berlin Woodwinds (piccolo, flutes)
Berlin Brass (horns, trumpets, trombones, bass trombone, tuba)
Spitfire Brass (cimbasso)
CinePerc (cymbals, surdos, monster low hits, tickies, frame drums, doumbek)
Deep Percussion Beds 2
Voxos choir
CinePiano
CineHarp
Tina Guo solo cello
Berlin strings
Spitfire Symphonic Strings

Recorded in StaffPad, mixed in Cubase

Usage

How might a cue like this be used? As suggested by the title, human struggle overcoming insurmountable challenges. The cue builds and builds with a huge payoff. This could be used in any type of montage where all seems hopeless but finally reaches the goal: sports, invention, love... you name it, this would fit in numerous situations.

Metadata

When creating metadata for the cue to help identify the music's characteristics you might include descriptions such as:

Celebratory, determined, feel good, glorious, motivational, optimistic, triumphant, etc.

No Mountain Too High

Composed and Orchestrated by
Steve Barden

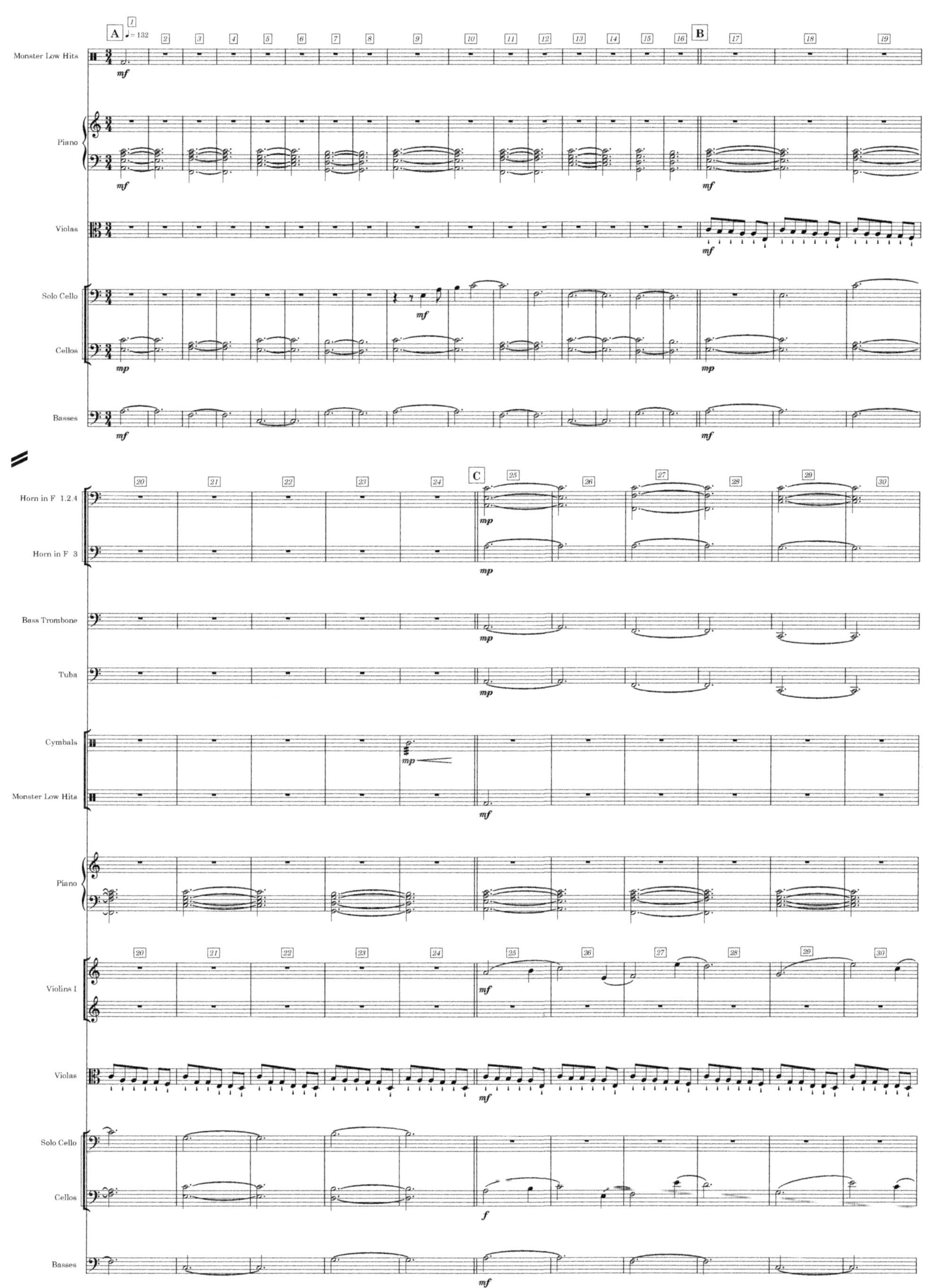

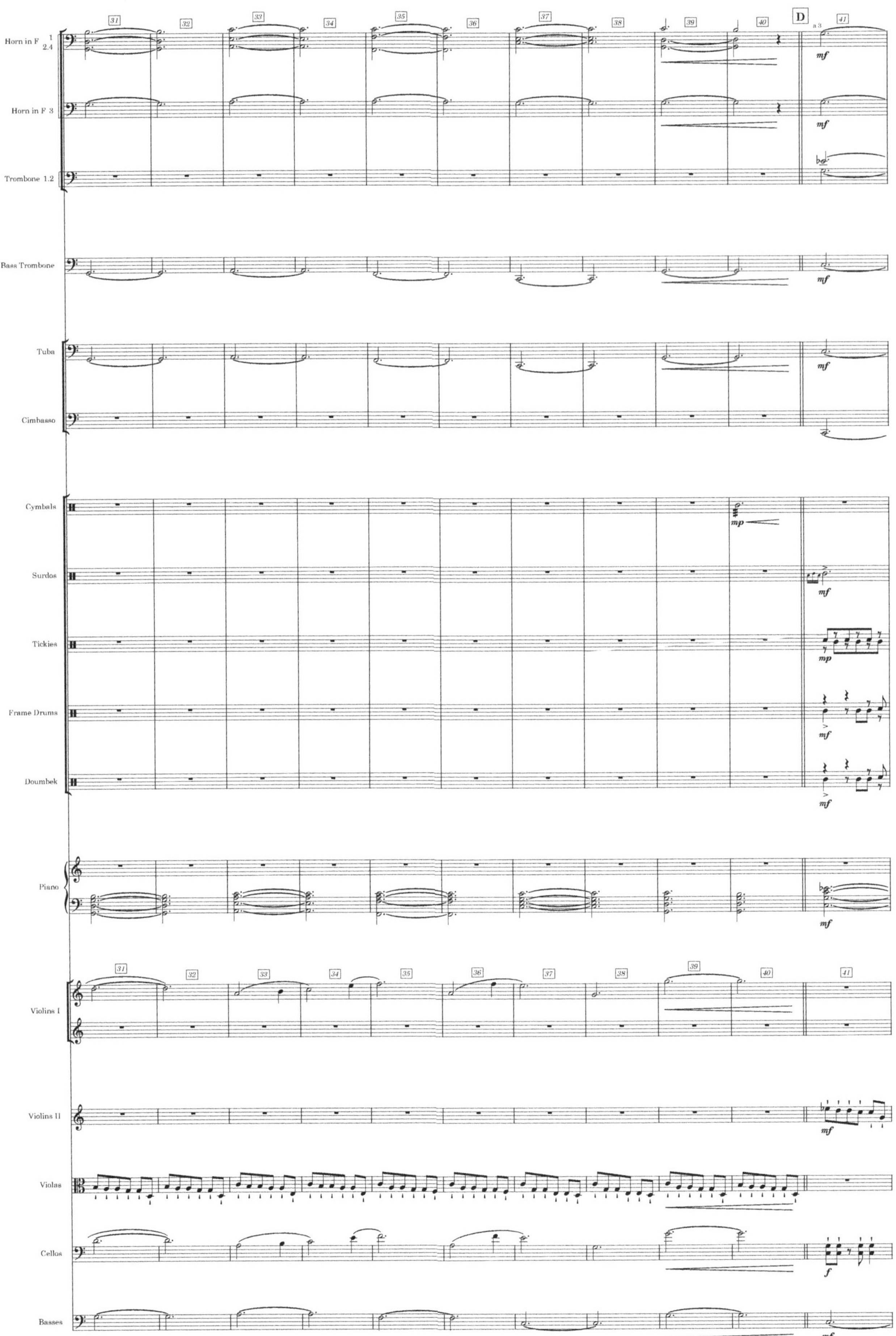
Horn in F 1 2.4
Horn in F 3
Trombone 1.2
Bass Trombone
Tuba
Cimbasso
Cymbals
Surdos
Tickies
Frame Drums
Doumbek
Piano
Violins I
Violins II
Violas
Cellos
Basses
D
a 3
mf
mp
f

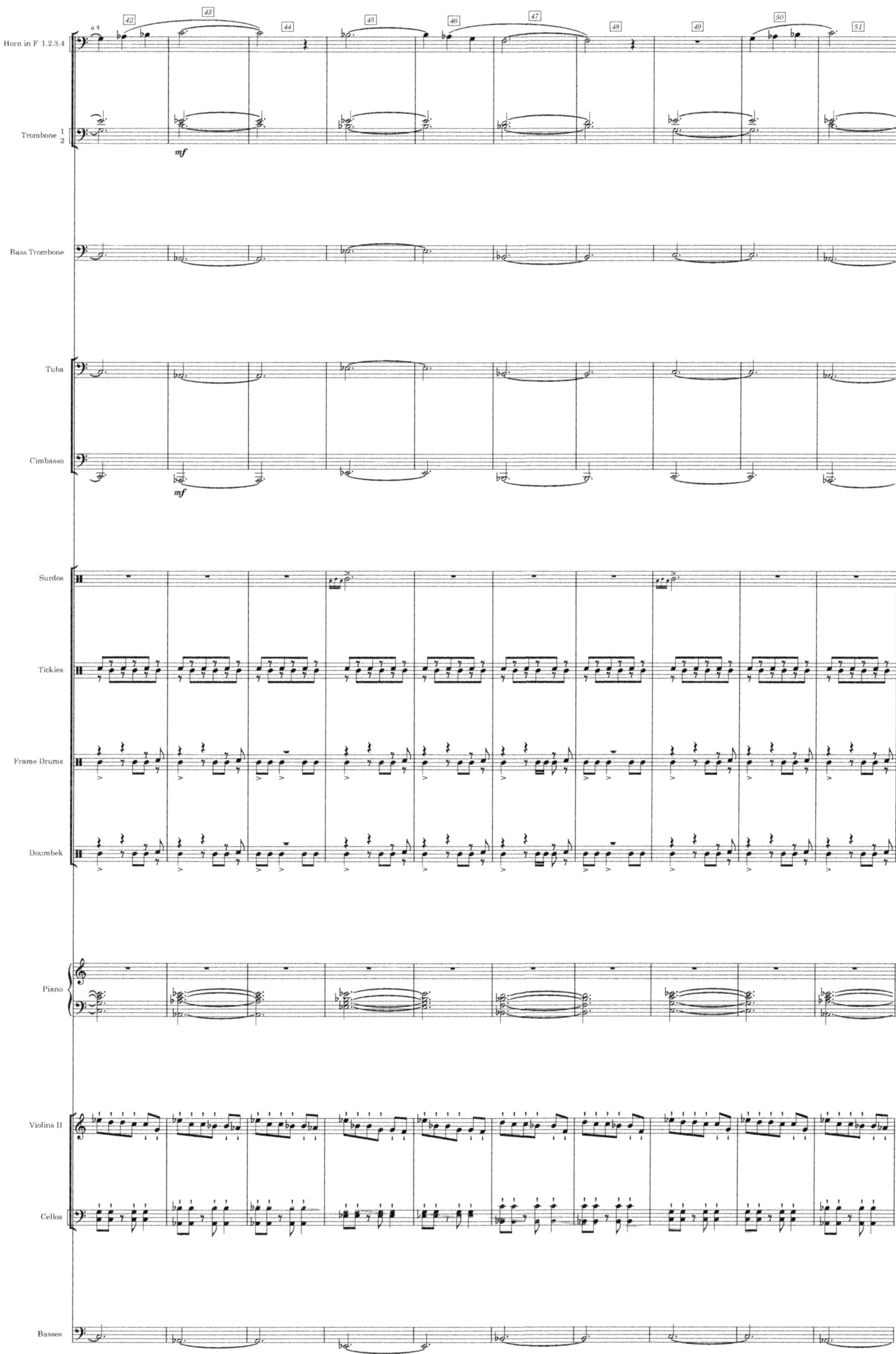
a 4
42
43
44
45
46
47
48
49
50
51
Horn in F 1.2.3.4
Trombone 1 2
mf
Bass Trombone
Tuba
Cimbasso
mf
Surdos
Tickies
Frame Drums
Doumbek
Piano
Violins II
Cellos
Basses

Piccolo
Flute 1.2
Horn in F 1.2.3.4
Trumpet in B♭ 1.2
Trumpet in B♭ 3
Trombone 1 2
Bass Trombone
Tuba
Cimbasso
Surdos
Tickies
Frame Drums
Doumbek
Choir
Piano
Violins I
Violins II
Violas
Cellos
Basses
E
52
53
54
55
56
57
58
59
60
61
a 4
a 2
1.2. a 2
3.4. a 2
mf
mp
f

62
63
64
65
66
67
68
69
70
71
72
Piccolo
Flute 1.2
a 2
1.2. a 2
Horn in F 1.2 3.4
3.4 a 2
Trumpet in B♭ 1 2
Trumpet in B♭ 3
Trombone 1 2
Bass Trombone
Tuba
Tickies
Frame Drums
Doumbek
Choir
Piano
Violins I
Violins II
Violas
Cellos
Basses

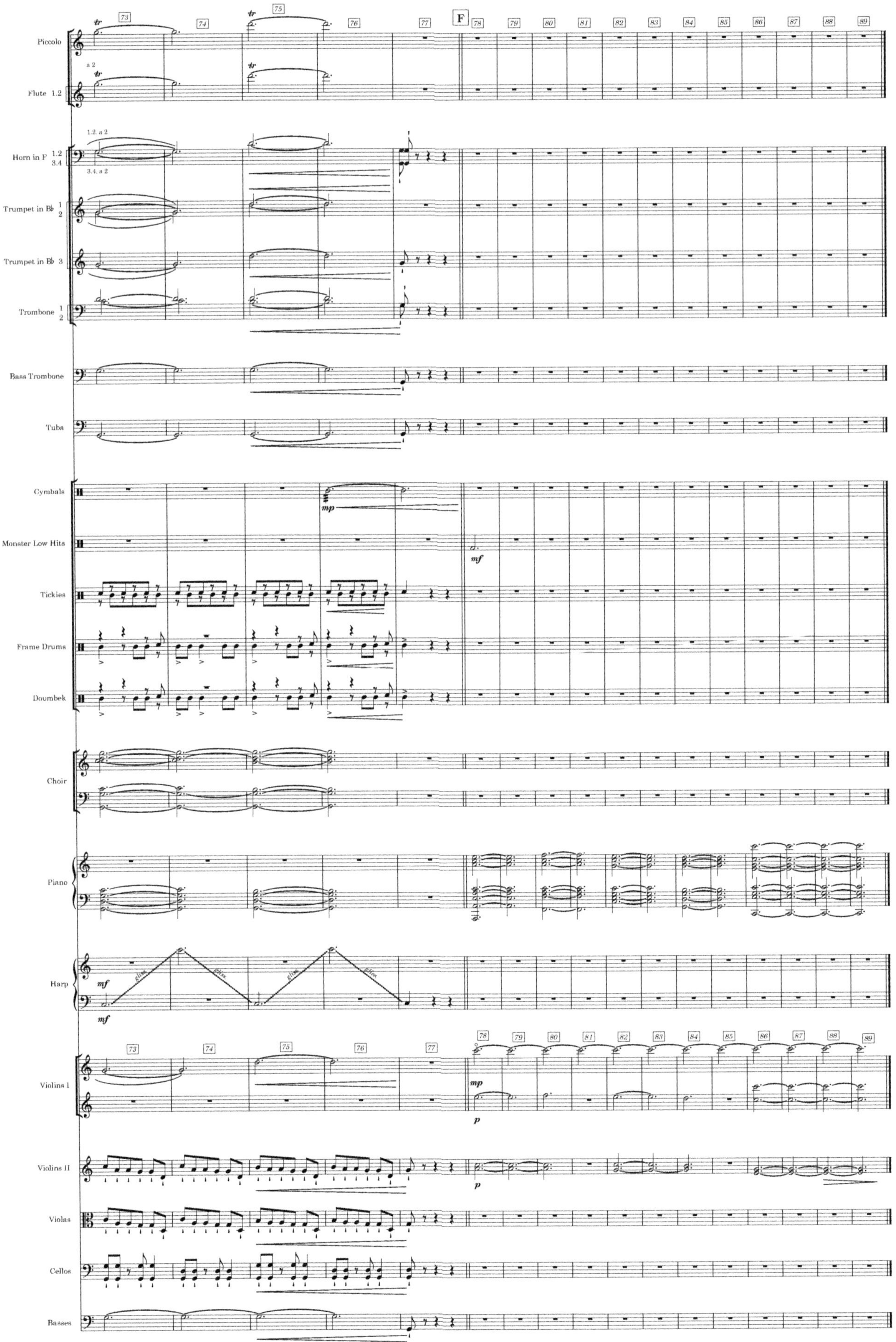
F
Piccolo
Flute 1.2
a 2
Horn in F 1.2 3.4
1.2. a 2
3.4. a 2
Trumpet in B♭ 1 2
Trumpet in B♭ 3
Trombone 1 2
Bass Trombone
Tuba
Cymbals
Monster Low Hits
Tickies
Frame Drums
Doumbek
Choir
Piano
Harp
gliss.
Violins I
Violins II
Violas
Cellos
Basses

Silly Willy

Tempo: 112 bpm

Key: C major

Track 6 - Silly Willy.mp3

As a child of the 1960s I grew up with the sound of Hanna-Barbera cartoons permeating my existence. Huckleberry Hound, Quick Draw McGraw, The Flintstones, Magilla Gorilla...the list goes on and on. *Silly Willy* is my homage to that sound.

While this style is specifically a cartoon sound, it is quite at home in reality television. The silliness of the music fits any scene that is comedic in nature.

The Hanna-Barbera sound, as defined by the legendary composer Hoyt Curtin, is made up of a rather small orchestra. This was probably not by choice but by budget limitations. Although the H-B orchestra usually also features a small string section, this cue includes no strings (except for the double bass).

Instruments featured include: 1 flute, 2 clarinets, 1 bass clarinet, 1 bassoon, 1 trumpet, 1 trombone, xylophone, snare drum, piano, harp, drum kit (cymbals only), and 1 double bass. One of the very distinctive sounds of this style is the trumpet playing with a Harmon mute and opening and closing the bell with a "wah-wah" effect. Woodwinds are the primary orchestral color with the xylophone emphasizing various passages.

The cue starts with a bouncy bassoon playing staccato notes. This gives the feeling of a goofy, silly character. The clarinets play the backbeat - the "pah" to the bassoon's "oom" to complete the "oom pah" figure. If played on a piano (left hand) this would be referred to as a *stride* pattern. This pattern is commonly found in polkas.

The bassoon opens the cue framing a chord progression of C major to F#(6) major with the clarinets filling out the chords. The non-diatonic movement from C to F# gives the piece a rather quirky feel, keeping the listener off balance.

Fig 1

The first melody seen is from the flute. In bar 6 the high C note on the flute is the diminished fifth (b5) of the F# chord. In bar 7 the melody moves from G down to F#. This F# note fits naturally on the F# chord, but as a standalone melody, it is diatonic until it hits the F# which is the augmented fourth (#4) of the C major scale. This puts the melody in a lydian mode. As we've seen from other cues in this volume, the lydian mode adds tension and fits the cinematic quality of the cue.

Fig 2

The trumpet answers the flute melody with a couple of simple notes. The trumpet is muted with a Harmon mute. A "wah-wah" effect is made by opening and closing the bell of the mute with the player's hand. As mentioned earlier, this sound is one of the characteristic sounds in Hanna-Barbera cartoons. This orchestral color will be used throughout the cue playing simple countermelodies.

Fig 3

There are numerous *stops* where the music hits a break point, and a comical fill takes place. In bar 13 the xylophone and piano play a quick sequence of sixteenth notes.

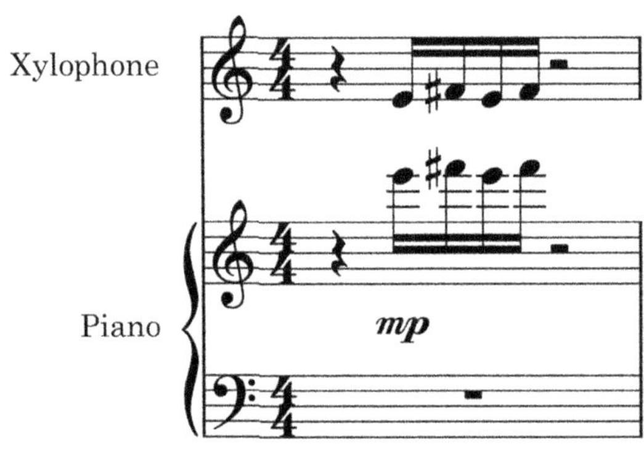

Fig 4

A similar fill occurs in bar 19, but this time it's the clarinets along with the xylophone.

Fig 5

Letter D begins the middle section (the B section) of the cue. Harmonically the chord progression is the same as before, C to F#, but the pattern will modulate going up in minor thirds. There is a comedic fill after each iteration of this figure.

Fig 6

At the end of this section the tempo ritards in bar 23 before returning to the original tempo. The cue then starts over. Letters E and F are the same as letters A and B. However, letter H introduces a new figure played by the clarinets and the xylophone, then adding the flute in bars 35 and 36.

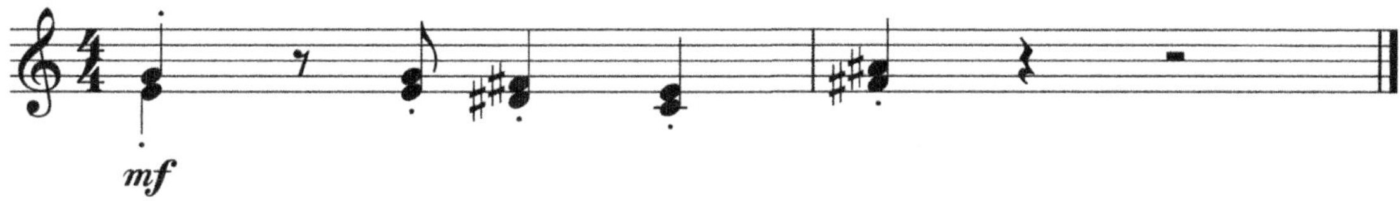

Fig 7

Letter H introduces a new melody played by the clarinets. Initially, in bar 37 both clarinets play a C major arpeggio, but in bar 39 the first clarinet moves up a half-step to Db. This creates a completely dissonant sound, but in this context, it fits the goofy quality of the cartoon sound.

Fig 8

Finally, letter I takes us out with the original melodies, but the flutes now play additional fills and the xylophone adds an ostinato pattern:

Fig 9

Virtual Instruments

For this recording I utilized the following instruments:

CineWinds (flute, clarinets, bass clarinet, bassoon)
CinePerc (xylophone)
ProjectSam Animator
ProjectSam Swing More! (double bass)

Recorded in Cubase

Usage

How might a cue like this be used? Obviously, this will sit well with many types of animation. But reality television makes use of many types of "wacky" music whenever they wish to portray a character that is clueless, stupid, silly, etc. A cue like this should find numerous uses.

Metadata

When creating metadata for the cue to help identify the music's characteristics you might include descriptions such as:

Cartoony, comical, drunk, fun, humorous, silly, slapstick, zany, etc.

Silly Willy

Composed and Orchestrated by
Steve Barden

rallentando.......a tempo
Clarinet in B♭ 1.2
Bass Clarinet in B♭
Bassoon
Trumpet in B♭
Trombone
Xylophone
Drum Kit
Piano
Hp
gliss.
Upright Bass
E
F
G
Flute

34
35
36
H
37
38
39
40
Flute
Clarinet in B♭ 1.2
Bassoon
Trumpet in B♭
Trombone
Xylophone
Snare Drum
Upright Bass
mf
mp
tr

I
41
42
43
44
45
46
Flute
Clarinet in B♭ 1
Clarinet in B♭ 2
Bassoon
Trumpet in B♭
Xylophone
Upright Bass
mf
mp

47
48
49
50
51
52
Flute
Clarinet in B♭ 1.2
Bassoon
Trumpet in B♭
Xylophone
Upright Bass

At the Casino

Tempo: 120 bpm

Key: A minor

Track 7 - At the Casino.mp3

In spite of the jazz vibe, this cue is a *dramedy* cue. The defining colors of dramedy music are pizzicato strings, mallet instruments (xylophone, marimba, vibes, glockenspiel), and percussion. As long as you adhere to this fundamental sound set you can pretty much create any style of music and it will fit in the genre of dramedy music which is the primary sound used in reality television.

At the Casino is fundamentally jazz. I envisioned it being used to set the backdrop of a James Bond-style story while the main character sits around the baccarat table drinking a shaken-not-stirred martini. I modeled the orchestral colors to that of a 1960s Henry Mancini score: alto flutes, French horns, strings, and bongos. There is something about adding bongos to lift a cue like this up.

The cue begins with the low strings (viola, cello, bass) playing the pizzicato rhythmic figure that will persist throughout the piece.

Fig 1

The chord progression in these first four bars is Am - Am - Bb7 - Bb7. This will be an eight-bar phrase. The last four bars of the phrase are Am - Am - F7 / E7 - Am. This is very similar to a minor blues chord progression. In a blues progression you would see a Dm instead of the Bb7 chord. The primary difference between Dm and Bb7 (not counting the root note) is the Ab (instead of A) note which adds tension to the sound. For me, the Bb7 chord is what gives this cue its cool sound.

The melody is played by a trio of alto flutes. The alto flute is synonymous with cool/jazz/spy scoring. Henry Mancini's *Pink Panther* theme is the epitome of how to use the alto flute in this context.

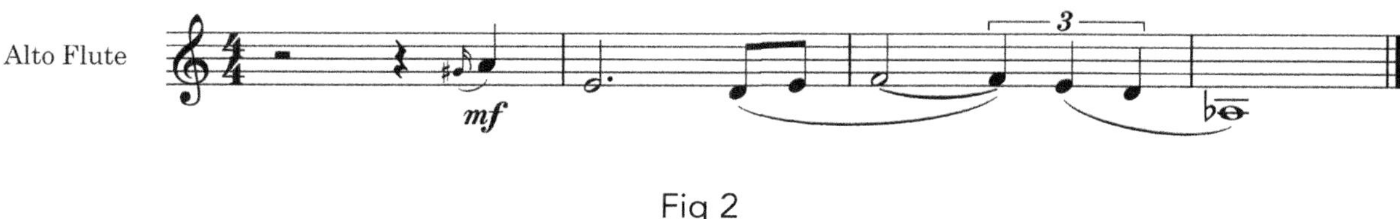

Fig 2

Letter B continues as a repeat of letter A. We add a shaker, bongos, and the violins playing a pad.

Fig 3

We also add the mallet instruments: marimba and vibraphone. The marimba doubles the melody playing an octave higher, and the vibes add a very cool color to the sound with simple chordal notes. Although the vibraphone part is simple, the sound of this instrument puts the stamp on the cool jazz sound.

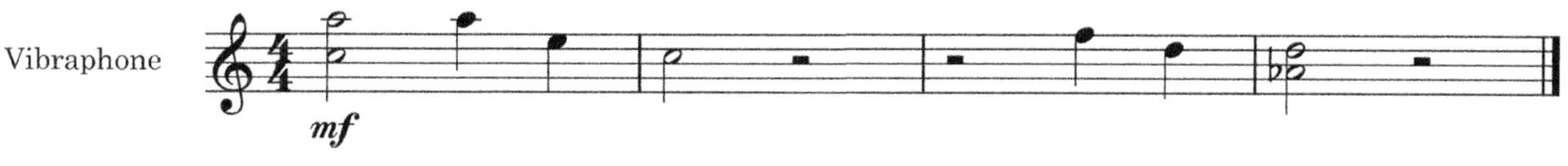

Fig 4

Letter C is the B section - the bridge of the piece - by shifting the key to D minor. The chord progression for the next eight bars is Dm - Dm - Am - Am - Dm - Dm - B7(!) - E7. The B7 leading to the E7 is the *V of V* leading to the V chord (the E7). This type of turnaround can be found in any music theory book (secondary dominant pattern) and adds a simple but effective voice leading to resolve the chords leading back to the original key of A minor.

The violins and alto flutes play a melody of chromatic movement that is so familiar in the spy genre.

Fig 5

Letter D and E are simply a repeat of letter B where the complete orchestra continues till the end. There is a nice button ending where that final phrase is repeated once again, then briefly holds out the last note before hitting the final chord.

Fig 6

Virtual Instruments

For this recording I utilized the following instruments:

CineWinds (alto flute)
Berlin Woodwinds (alto flute)
StaffPad (alto flute)
Berlin Brass (French horns)
Spitfire Percussion (shaker)
CinePerc (marimba, vibraphone, bongos)
Spitfire Symphonic Strings

Recorded in StaffPad, mixed in Cubase

Usage

How might a cue like this be used? As stated earlier this checks all the boxes of a spy score. Because it's a jazz cue it could easily be used as source music played in a restaurant or casino or bar. The cue would also fit nicely to frame a murder mystery-style show. Lots of tension is suggested by the minor chord progression.

Metadata

When creating metadata for the cue to help identify the music's characteristics you might include descriptions such as:

Cool, confident, dangerous, intrigue, mysterious, secretive, sneaky, etc.

At the Casino

Composed and Orchestrated by
Steve Barden

Alto Flute in G 1.2
Alto Flute in G 3
Horn in F 1.2.4
3
Shak.
Bon. 1
Bon. 2
Marimba
Vibraphone
Violins I
Violins II
Violas
Cellos
Basses in C
C
a 3
1.
2.3. a 2
mf
mp
13
14
15
16
17
18

Alto Flute in G 1
2
Alto Flute in G 3
Horn in F 1.2.4
3
Shak.
Bon. 1
Bon. 2
Marimba
Vibraphone
Violins I
Violins II
Violas
Cellos
Basses in C
1.
2.3. a 2
a 3
19
20
21
22
23

Alto Flute in G 1.2
Alto Flute in G 3
Horn in F 1.2.4 3
Shak.
Bon. 1
Bon. 2
Marimba
Vibraphone
Violins I
Violins II
Violas
Cellos
Basses in C
D
24
25
26
27
28
a 3
mp
mf

Alto Flute in G 1.2
Alto Flute in G 3
Horn in F 1.2.4 3
Shak.
Bon. 1
Bon. 2
Marimba
Vibraphone
Violins I
Violins II
Violas
Cellos
Basses in C
E
29
30
31
32
33
34
a 3
mp
mf

a 3
35
36
37
38
39
40
Alto Flute in G 1.2
Alto Flute in G 3
Horn in F 1.2.4
3
1.2.4. a 3
Shak.
mf
Bon. 1
Bon. 2
Marimba
Vibraphone
Violins I
Violins II
Violas
Cellos
Basses in C

a 3
41
42
Alto Flute in G 1.2
Alto Flute in G 3
Horn in F 1.2.4
3
Shak.
Bon. 1
Bon. 2
Marimba
Vibraphone
Violins I
Violins II
Violas
Cellos
Basses in C

On the Move

Tempo: 140 bpm

Key: Bb major

Track 8 - On the Move.mp3

On the Move is a dramedy cue. The defining colors of dramedy music are pizzicato strings, mallet instruments (xylophone, marimba, vibraphone, glockenspiel), and percussion. This cue checks all of these boxes. At a tempo of 140 bpm this cue is full of frenetic energy.

Except for the first violins the entire string section plays pizzicato the entire time. The bass plays a strict quarter-note pattern while the rest of the group (2nd violins, violas, and celli) play the up-beat of the chords.

Fig 1

The melody is primarily covered by the marimba and doubled by the first violins. The marimba is a very common melody instrument in the dramedy genre. The key is Bb major and the first chord is Bb, however, the melody begins on the flatted 3rd, Db (written as C# to avoid unnecessary accidentals). This immediately gives the piece instant tension that wants to be resolved to the D note. The flatted third is a *blue* note, common in blues scales.

Fig 2

The second bar of the melody is highlighted by the flutes doubling an octave higher. This melody follows a common pattern of jazz playing: The Bb chord is outlined in descending notes (F, D, Bb), however, each note is approached a half-step below. E to F, C# to D, followed by the resolution of the root Bb. Just like the melody in the first measure, this half-step approach gives it instant tension begging each note to be resolved.

Fig 3

In addition to the flutes doubling the melody of the *statement* (marimba) & *answer* (flutes), the high woodwinds (piccolo, flutes, oboe, and clarinet) add additional excitement by playing rapid flourishes, This technique is used frequently by John Williams in many of his fast-action cues.

Fig 4

A shaker is the first rhythm instrument appearing right from the beginning of the cue playing a sixteenth-note pattern. Bongos join in starting in bar 9 for the second iteration of the "A" theme.

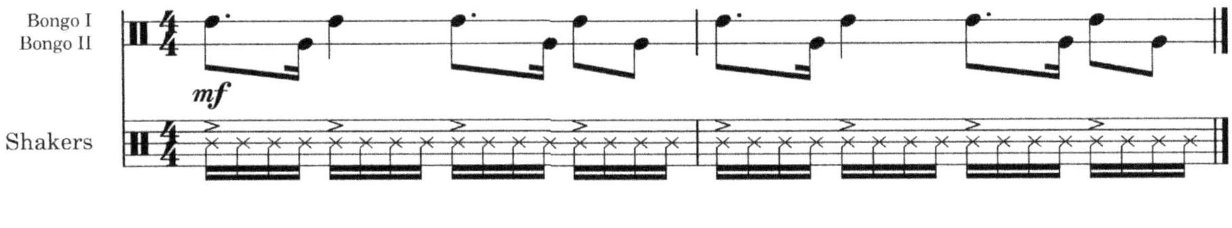

Fig 5

The "B" theme enters at letter C. Here the pizzicato continues with the same rhythmic pattern, but the melody is picked up now by the xylophone doubled by bowed, staccato first violins. This is a very fast pattern of sixteenth notes. This only helps keep up the frantic pace of the cue.

Fig 6

Just as the flutes helped the marimba in the opening melody, the piccolo and trumpet assist the xylophone by adding a three-note sixteenth note phrase in its second bar (bar 18), as well as bars 20-22.

Fig 7

The final A section begins at letter D. This is a recap of the first A section, but now we add some additional percussion sounds to add to the wackiness of the cue. We'll hear the guiro in bars 25 and 27, wood blocks in bars 37-40 followed by temple blocks taking over in bars 41-43, and the glockenspiel highlighting melody notes starting in bar 37. The simple addition of these percussion sounds helps insure the development of the cue and avoids a staleness of simply repeating what we heard in the first A section.

Virtual Instruments

For this recording I utilized the following instruments:

Spitfire Woodwinds (piccolo)

Berlin Woodwinds (flutes, oboe, clarinet, bassoons)

CineBrass (trumpet, trombone)

CinePerc (timpani, glockenspiel, snare drum, xylophone, marimba, bongos, wood blocks, temple blocks, guiro)

Spitfire Percussion (shaker)

Spitfire Symphonic Strings

Recorded in StaffPad, mixed in Cubase

Usage

How might a cue like this be used? This type of cue will find lots of opportunities in reality television. The frantic pace of the music will give any scene a sense of urgency. It evokes silliness and is guaranteed to make you smile.

Metadata

When creating metadata for the cue to help identify the music's characteristics you might include descriptions such as:

Cartoony, comical, silly, vigorous, chaotic, energetic, frantic, hi-energy, mischievous, nervous, etc.

On the Move

Composed and Orchestrated by
Steve Barden

B
6
7
8
9
10
11
12
13
14
Piccolo
Flute 1.2.3
Oboe
Clarinet in B♭
Bassoon 1.2
Trumpet in B♭
Marimba
Bon. 1
Bon. 2
Shakers
Violins I
Violins II
Violas
Cellos
Basses in C
a 2
a 3
1.2.
3.
mf
Violins II
Flute 1.2 3
7

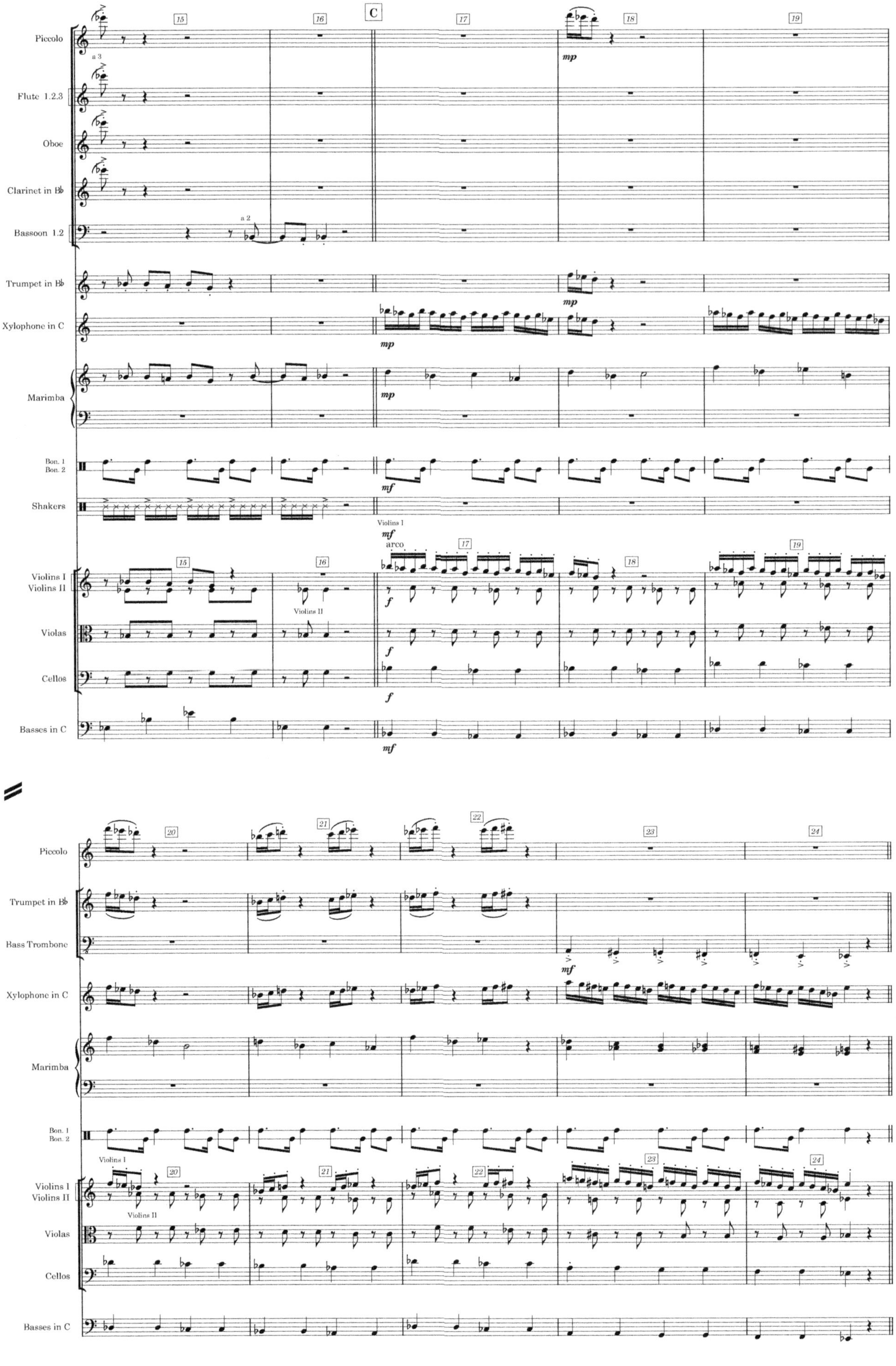

C

Piccolo
Flute 1.2.3
Oboe
Clarinet in B♭
Bassoon 1.2
Trumpet in B♭
Xylophone in C
Marimba
Bon. 1
Bon. 2
Shakers
Violins I
Violins II
Violas
Cellos
Basses in C

D
Piccolo
Flute 1.2.3
Oboe
Clarinet in B♭
Bassoon 1.2
Marimba
Guiro
Shakers
pizz.
Violins I
Violins II
Violas
Cellos
Basses in C
E
Trumpet in B♭
Bon. 1
Bon. 2

Piccolo
Flute 1.2 3
Oboe
Clarinet in B♭
Bassoon 1.2
Trumpet in B♭
Glockenspiel in C
Marimba
Bon. 1 Bon. 2
Wood Blocks
Shakers
Violins I Violins II
Violas
Cellos
Basses in C
35
36
37
38
1.
2.3. a 2
a 2
a 3
7
mf
mp
Violins II

Piccolo
Flute 1.2.3
Oboe
Clarinet in B♭
Bassoon 1.2
Trumpet in B♭
Timpani
Glockenspiel in C
Snare Drum
Marimba
Bon. 1
Bon. 2
Wood Blocks
T. Bl.
Shakers
Violins I
Violins II
Violas
Cellos
Basses in C
39
40
41
42
43
44
45
a 3
a 2
1.2.
3.
1.
7
mf
mp

Countdown to Zero Hour

Tempo: 120 bpm

Key: C major

Track 9 - Countdown to Zero Hour.mp3

A straight-up dramedy cue, *Countdown to Zero Hour* features all of the required instruments to be considered dramedy: pizzicato strings, mallet instruments (xylophone, glockenspiel, marimba, vibraphone), and percussion. This cue also features woodwinds but no brass.

Since the days of *Desperate Housewives*, the dramedy sound quite often suggested "sneaking around." This cue depicts that type of scene, particularly in the middle, B-section (bars 23-30). The rest of the cue, the A sections depict more of an uneasy feeling, waiting for something to happen: something probably not good.

The track opens with the tick-tock sound of a marimba alternating root-fifth (C - G) depicting either the ticking of a clock (suggesting a passage of time) or perhaps even a heartbeat.

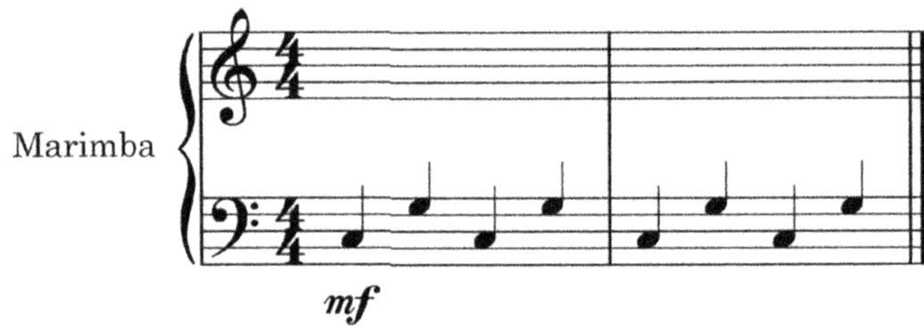

Fig 1

The melody introduced by the woodwinds: 3 flutes and 2 clarinets playing in octaves.

Fig 2

In the key of C major, the melody often slips down to an F# note. As with many other cues in this collection, this augmented fourth puts the melody in a lydian mode. This is a common cinematic approach and gives the music additional tension.

The initial melody lasts four measures but adds an additional measure of no-melody before returning. This "breath" adds to the mounting tension and uncertainty. When the melody begins again in bar 8, a shaker is added to give the piece motion.

Fig 3

The same bar of silence (no melody) occurs again at bar 12 before starting the next A section (letter B, bar 13). The form of the cue is A-A-B-A-A. This is essentially an A-B-A form where the A sections are doubled in length. For this next A section we introduce the pizzicato strings. The low strings, bass and cello, play single notes at the beginning of each bar. The second violins and violas play an eighth note figure that supports the woodwinds melody notes.

Fig 4

In addition, we add a vibraphone doubling the chords of the marimba. The vibes have the tremolo motor running. We also add djembe drums for added movement.

Fig 5

In bars 18-22, the flutes play the melody up an octave. This adds more energy to the piece. We also add the first violins playing tremolo notes to increase the uneasy feeling.

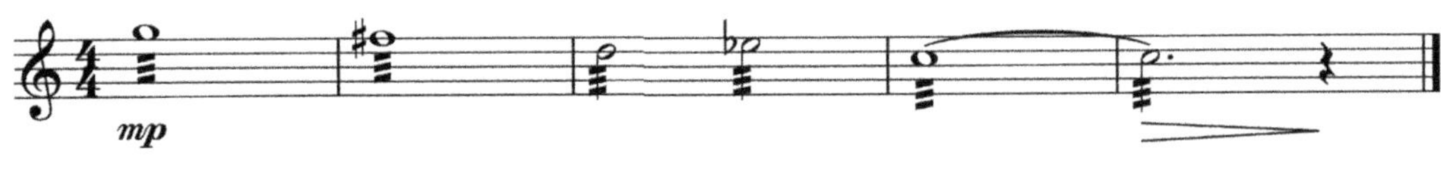

Fig 6

We finally get to the B section (letter C) at bar 23. The cellos and violas have switched to arco bowing and double the part with the bass clarinet and bassoon.

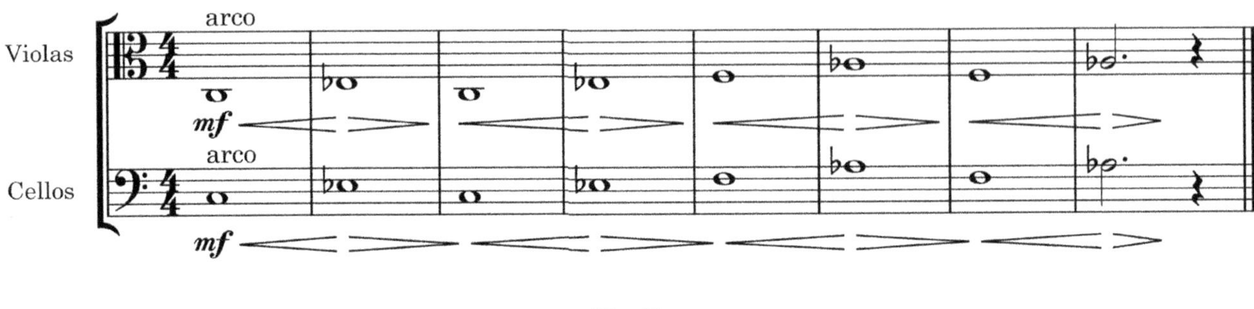

Fig 7

This figure of whole notes rises and lowers in volume to mimic the shape of the melody of the flutes (doubled by the glockenspiel).

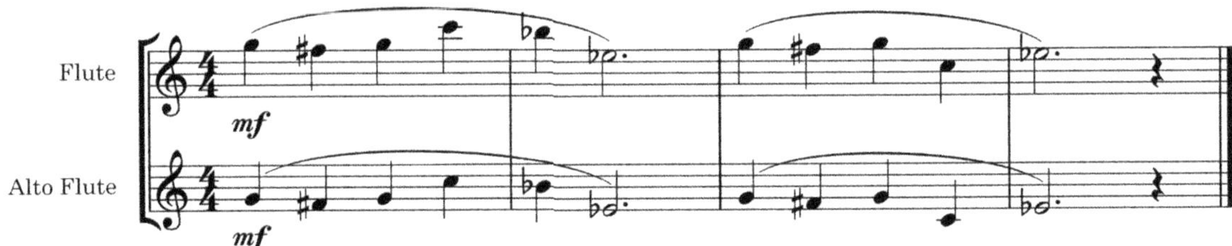

Fig 8

When the A section returns (letter D, bar 31), the clarinets drop out and the flutes are harmonized instead of playing in octaves. This is a way to keep the cue from sounding too repetitive while changing the tonal color, even briefly.

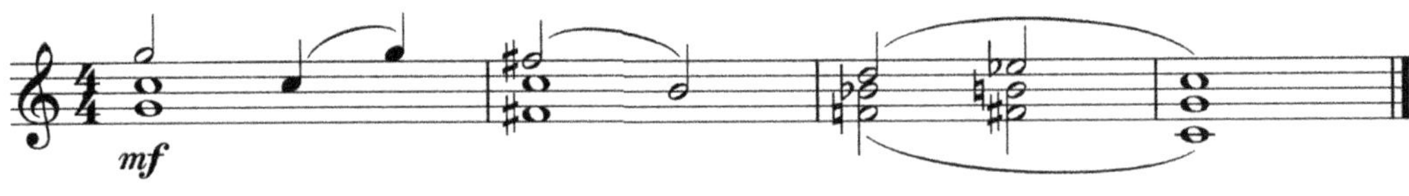

Fig 9

The rest of the cue will follow the same arrangement as we saw earlier in the piece.

Virtual Instruments

For this recording I utilized the following instruments:

Berlin Woodwinds (flutes, alto flute, clarinets, bass clarinet, bassoon)
CinePerc (shaker, xylophone, glockenspiel, marimba, vibraphone, djembe)
Spitfire Symphonic Strings

Recorded in StaffPad, mixed in Cubase

Usage

How might a cue like this be used? Every reality program in existence has used cues like this one. Whenever a character has any self-doubt you will hear similar cues. There is much anticipation happening here. Not knowing what's going to happen next. The ticking clock sound of the marimba drives this point home. The melody is not overbearing but adds a strong sense of anxiety. Even without the shaker and drums this cue will still convey the same emotion.

Metadata

When creating metadata for the cue to help identify the music's characteristics you might include descriptions such as:

Anxious, depressed, doubtful, foreboding, nervous, reflective, tense, thinking, worried, etc.

Countdown to Zero Hour

Composed and Orchestrated
Steve Barden

Flute 1 2.3
Clarinet in B♭ 1.2
Shakers
Xylophone in C
Marimba
Vibraphone
Djembe
Violins I
Violins II
Violas
Cellos
Basses in C
17
18
19
20
21
22
mp

C
Flute 1 2.3
Alto Flute in G
Bass Clarinet in B♭
Bassoon
Glockenspiel in C
Marimba
Vibraphone
Violas
Cellos
Basses in C
arco
mf
mp
23
24
25
26
27
28
29

D
30
31
32
33
34
35
36
37
38
1.
mf
2.3.
Flute 1 2.3
Alto Flute in G
Bass Clarinet in B♭
Bassoon
Shakers
Glockenspiel in C
Marimba
Vibraphone
Violas
Cellos
Basses in C

E
39
40
41
42
43
44
45
1.
mf
2.3. a 2
a 2
p
Violins II
pizz.
Flute 1 2.3
Clarinet in B♭ 1.2
Shakers
Xylophone in C
Marimba
Vibraphone
Djembe
Violins I Violins II
Violas
Basses in C

46
47
48
49
50
Flute 1.2
3
Clarinet in B♭ 1.2
a 2
Shakers
Xylophone in C
Marimba
Vibraphone
Djembe
Violins I
Violins II
Violas
Cellos
pizz.
mf
Basses in C

Acknowledgements

This book is the result of years of study, composing a lot of bad music, making a ton of mistakes, and being honest with myself as to what constitutes good music. But the journey did not happen without the help, guidance, and inspiration from many, many people.

I want to acknowledge those that I've worked with over the years in the production music (music library) field. In one way or another they were able to guide me, prod me, or otherwise cajole me into not settling for subpar music. In particular I wish to thank Chuck Henry, Chuck Schlacter, Kevin Kiner, Joy Basu, Ryan Sager, David Trotter, John Fulford, and Volker Barber.

My friends in the L.A. Taxi Hang for continued support and inspiration: Matt, Tracey & Vance, Stan, Lew, Paula, Jacqueline, Cisko, Brian, Tamara, Robin, Charity, Juliet, Nitanee, Cher, John, Trevor, Elizabeth, Al, Jeanna, Carrie, Angela, Steve C, Steve G, Frank, and Bolt.

Thanks to Michael Laskow of Taxi A&R for continuing to create a space for composers to learn the craft of writing production music.

Thanks to the many instructors from back in the days of the UCLA Film Scoring extension program. Their guidance set me on my path to writing music for media: Mark Watters, Don B. Ray, Gerald Fried, Joe E. Rand, Ray Colcord, Charles Bernstein.

Finally, a big thanks once again to my publisher Ron Middlebrook for coming up with the idea which turned into this book.

About the Author

Steve Barden is a production music composer for film and television. His music can be heard on television somewhere in the world on a daily basis. His music has aired on ABC, CBS, NBC, FOX, CW, ABC Family, A&E, American Heroes Channel, Animal Planet, Biography Channel, Bravo, The Cooking Channel, Discovery Channel, E!, Food Network, Game Show Network, HGTV, Investigation Discovery, Lifetime, MTV, National Geographic Channel, Oprah Winfrey Network, Outdoor Channel, Oxygen, PBS, Science Channel, Style Channel, SyFy Channel, TLC, Travel Channel, truTV, Univision, and VH1.

Steve is a multi-instrumentalist playing guitar, piano, and violin. He has studied guitar at the Guitar Institute of Technology in Hollywood (currently Musician's Institute) and studied film scoring at UCLA. He has scored animated television series *Tic Tac Toons, Journey to the Heart of the World*, and *Button Nose.* He also scored the award winning animated short, *The Baseball Card Shop*, originally produced by Nickelodeon. He has also written jingles and theme songs for Los Angeles radio personalities, *Mark & Brian*, and also *Kevin & Bean*.

Steve is a husband, father, grandfather, and cat guardian. He lives in Lakewood, California with his wife, Leanne, and an undisclosed number of cats.

You can find Steve Barden online at his website, www.stevebarden.com.

More Great Books from Steve Barden...

WRITING PRODUCTION MUSIC FOR TV

The Road to Success

by Steve Barden, foreword by Kevin Kiner

This complete guide for any composer interested in earning money writing music for television is aimed at the complete novice as well as the seasoned expert. It leads you through the steps necessary to succeed in the music business: finding music libraries; submitting music; joining a Performance Rights Organization; understanding contracts; keeping organized; networking; and even revealing how much money you can earn.

00252427 .... $29.99

MASTERING STAFFPAD

Digital Music Notation for the Modern Composer

by Steve Barden, foreword by David William Hearn

Mastering StaffPad - Digital Music Notation for the Modern Composer is a complete reference guide for the music notation and composition app available for Microsoft Surface and Apple iPad tablets. This phenomenal app allows you to write music notation naturally - as if it were pencil and paper! - and hear back your compositions in all its glory with professional music sound libraries.

00354792 .... $29.99

You'll like what you hear!

P.O. Box 17878 - Anaheim Hills, CA 92817

(714) 779-9390 centerstrm@aol.com | www.centerstream-usa.com